Digital Assurance

Paul Gerrard is a consultant, teacher, author, webmaster, developer, tester, conference speaker, rowing coach and a publisher. He has conducted consulting assignments in all aspects of software testing and quality assurance, specialising in test assurance. He has presented keynote talks and tutorials at testing conferences across Europe, the USA, Australia, South Africa and occasionally won awards for them.

Educated at the universities of Oxford and Imperial College London, in 2010, Paul won the Eurostar European Testing Excellence Award and in 2013, won The European Software Testing Awards (TESTA) Lifetime Achievement Award.

In 2002, Paul wrote, with Neil Thompson, "Risk-Based E-Business Testing". Paul wrote "The Tester's Pocketbook" in 2009. Paul co-authored with Susan Windsor "The Business Story Pocketbook" in 2011 and wrote "Lean Python" in 2014. In 2014, Paul was the Programme Chair for the EuroSTAR Conference in Dublin.

He is Principal of Gerrard Consulting Limited, Director of TestOpera Limited and is the host of the Assurance Leadership Forum in the UK.

Digital Assurance

Testing in the New Digital Age

Paul Gerrard

With a foreword by Jonathon Wright

The Tester's Press
Macclesfield UK

First published in Great Britain in 2017 by
THE TESTER'S PRESS
Silvaplana
35 Higher Fence Road
Macclesfield
Cheshire SK10 1QF
United Kingdom
Web: testers-press.com

CABook161219

Typeset by Paul Gerrard
Printed and bound by Lulu.com

Contents

Foreword

In the digital economy, every business is a software business, and the software landscape is changing forever. The traditional Core IT approach to providing business value through lengthy plan-build-test-deploy cycles can no longer deliver value in an increasingly competitive, consumer-centric landscape. Merely compressing these cycles through adopting iterative or agile methods does not address the challenges organisations face in terms of innovation, speed to market, quality and resilience.

Shifting to an Adaptive IT model calls for a new practice that requires accelerated communication, collaboration, integration, measurement and automation. Whether you label this as Digital Transformation, understanding the detail of this journey is an essential part of every organisation's journey to becoming a Digital Enterprise.

Here's the definition of Digital Enterprise based on my industry experience whilst delivering Digital Solutions across the globe:

> "The digitalization of processes, behaviours and interactions, resulting in continuously, adaptive, cognitive, innovative, business models."

Expanding the definition provides context behind the key digital terminology:

- Digitalisation process (digital engineering)

- Behaviours (algorithmic-business)

- Interactions (autonomous-business)

- Continuous (insight-driven (prescriptive & predictive))

- Adaptive (multi-modal delivery)

- Cognitive (adoption of Artificial Intelligence & Machine Learning)
- Innovative (smart & differentiated solutions)
- Business Models:
  - digital by default (LeanDX/start-up)
  - digital by design (DesignOps).

In this book Paul Gerrard explores the concepts behind Digital Assurance. These are critical success factors for any journey to Digital Transformation. Digital Assurance breaks down the silos across the entire organisation and allows all parties to get involved in exploiting their digital capabilities.

He will also introduce the concepts that surround Digital Governance capabilities to support complex 'ecosystems of ecosystems' to visualize the applications landscape and leverage connected intelligence to overlay business risk and providing both predictive and prescriptive insight into the behaviours of systems (both systemic and epistemic).

This book directly addresses the new delivery paradigm; from 'ideation' to design, development, testing through to operations (known as DesignOps) to provide a value-driven approach that is scalable when defining, building and deploying solutions.

Paul also explores the Digital Engineering practices (DevOps, Automation and Lean Engineering) by utilising these heuristics to simplify decision making across the continuous pipeline understanding the abiotic components of an environment and the interactions between systems of systems - the Digital Ecosystem (see page 4).

For some customers, these landscapes equate to hundreds if not thousands of upstream and downstream applications, endpoints and nodes (organisms) within ecosystems of ecosystems. Therefore, there is limited governance (archology) for representing chaotic, complex and complicated landscapes (archaeology).

CA technologies commit to continuously improve our leading-edge Solutions and Systems Thinking. We are constantly adapting our customer-centric solutions to align with maturing and emerging markets as part of our customers' journey to Digital Assurance.

Jonathon Wright is Director of Digital Assurance at CA.

Mail: jonathon.wright@ca.com
Twitter: @Jonathon_Wright
LinkedIn: https://www.linkedin.com/in/automation
slideshare.net/Jonathon_wright

Preface

What is Digital anyway?

The Digital phenomenon that is sweeping through business and the IT sector is the biggest thing since the Internet took the world by storm in the early 1990s. Unlike the Internet revolution and DotCom madness, Digital is largely business-driven. In that respect, there has been no slow-start. It's gone from nowhere to every ambitious organisation in about three years I'd say.

Today, just about every large organisation and many SMEs have Chief Digital Officers or Digital Transformation leaders. Digital agencies are springing up everywhere and offer varying blends of marketing, IT development, outsourcing and business consulting services.

The Digital stampede is a combination of business transformation using IT and IT transformation using the methods of Continuous Delivery, Shift-Left, DevOps, Analytics and Data-Driven Software development. In this respect, you could say Digital represents a bringing-up-to-date of both Business and IT.

Now, if the scope of Digital spans all the new technologies including mobile, the Internet of Things (IoT), Drones, 3D and 4D[1] printing, Artificial Intelligence (AI) and Machine Learning, sensors and actuators of all descriptions and Virtual or Augmented Reality, then it really is – *everything*.

---

[1] Self-assembling 'printed' objects.

This combination of huge scope, business pressure and changing development approaches will pose a huge problem for most testing teams and testers. This book is an attempt to summarise the challenge and make some general recommendations for coping, thriving or surviving a once-in-a-career transformation.

> "Digital Assurance breaks down the silos across the entire organisation – allows everyone to get involved in evolving digital capability: connected intelligence maps the value steam mapping of business challenges and goals. This is a new way of IT delivery that allows for digital initiatives to be deployed at pace across the organisation but in a (relatively) stable and industrialized state – a willingness to 'fail forward'."
>
> Jonathon Wright

This book is aimed at testers requiring an overview of the challenge and Digital leaders and managers wanting to know how to shape the testing and assurance of their projects.

Structure

There are nine chapters, an Appendix and Index.

Chapter 1 introduces Digital – what it is, how complex it could be and the scope of risks we'll need to address.

Chapter 2 presents a summary of Digital Assurance from the process angle and sets the scene for Assurance in Digital projects.

Chapter 3 describes Digital Assurance and makes recommendations for the introduction of a new test discipline.

Chapter 4 explains how models are at the heart of testing and are an essential 'shorthand' for test design.

Chapter 5 describes the concept of Shift-Left and how testers need to grasp this opportunity to be more effective.

Chapter 6 outlines the DevOps and Continuous Delivery philosophy and how testing is critical to making it work.

Chapter 7 presents an architecture of the IoT and how the risk landscape has grown wider and deeper.

Chapter 8 introduces Test Analytics and how experimentation and systems development become data-driven.

Chapter 9 summarises the book and give pointers to the future of Digital Assurance.

An Appendix contains references to relevant websites, papers and books.

An Index is included at the end of the Pocketbook.

Feedback, please!

I am very keen to receive your feedback and experience to enhance the format and content of the book. Give me feedback and I'll acknowledge you in the next edition.

Any errors or omissions are my fault entirely. Please let me know how I can improve this Pocketbook. Email me at paul@gerrardconsulting.com with suggestions or errors.

Acknowledgements

For their helpful feedback, guidance and encouraging comments, I'd like to thank the people at CA Technologies in Eynsham – Huw Price, Georgina Tilby, Tom Pryce and Jonathon Wright for interesting chats and the foreword of course.

"Speak softly and carry a big stick; you will go far."
Theodore Roosevelt

"The only thing to do with good advice is pass it on. It is never any use to oneself."
Oscar Wilde

"Give a man a fish, and you'll feed him for a day. Teach a man to fish, and he'll buy a funny hat. Talk to a hungry man about fish, and you're a consultant."
Scott Adams (Dogbert)

"There are three rules for writing a good requirement. Unfortunately, no one knows what they are."
Paul (with a nod to W.S. Maugham).

1   What is Digital?

Revolution

If you are not working on a "Digital" project, the hype that surrounds the whole concept of Digital and that is bombarding business and IT professions appears off-putting to say the least. But it would be wrong to ignore it. The Digital Transformation programmes that many organisations are embarking on are affecting business across all industry and government sectors. There is no doubt that it also affects people in their daily lives.

That sounds like yet another hype-fuelled statement intended to get the attention. It is attention grabbing, but it's also true. The scope of Digital[2] is growing to encompass the entirety of IT related disciplines and business that depends on it: that is – all business.

It is becoming clear that the scope and scale of Digital will include all the traditional IT of the past, but when fully realised it will include the following too:

- The IoT – every device of interest or value in the world will become connected; sensors of all types and purpose will be connected – by the billion – to the internet.

- Autonomous vehicles – cars, planes, ships, drones, buses will become commonplace in the next ten years or so. Each

---

[2] From now on I'll use the word Digital to represent Digital Transformation, Projects and the wide range of disciplines required in the 'Digital World'.

will be a "place on the move", fully connected and communicating with its environment.

- Our home, workplace, public and private spaces will be connected. Our mobile, portable or wearable devices will interact with their environment and each other – without human intervention.

- Robots will take over more and more physical tasks and make some careers obsolete and humans redundant. Robots will clean the city, fight our wars and care for the elderly.

- Software in the form of 'bots' will be our guardian angel and a constant irritant – notifying us of the latest offers and opportunities as we traverse our Smart Cities[3].

- The systems we use will be increasingly intelligent, but AI won't be limited to corporates. Voice control may well be the preferred user-interface on many devices in the home and our car.

- The operations or 'Digital Storm' of commerce, government, medicine, the law and warfare will be transformed in the next few years. The lives of mid-21st century citizens could be very different from ours.

Motivation

Still not convinced that Digital will change the world we live in? The suggested scale of change is overwhelming. Why is this happening? Is it hype or is it truly the way the world is going?

---

[3] See for example, http://learn.hitachiconsulting.com/Engineering-the-New-Reality

The changes that are taking place really are significant because it appears that this decade – the 2010's – are the point at which several technological and social milestones are being reached. This decade is witness to some tremendous human and technological achievements.

1. One third of the world is connected; there are plans to connect the remaining two-thirds[4]
2. The range of small devices that can be assembled into useful things has exploded. Their costs are plummeting.
3. Local and low power networking technologies can connect these devices.
4. Artificial Intelligence which has promised so much for so many years is finally delivering in the form of Machine Learning.
5. Virtual and Augmented Reality-based systems are coming. Sony VR launched (13/10/2016) to over 1.8million people and Samsung VR starts at under $100.
6. Robotics, drone technology and 3D printing are now viable and workable whilst falling in cost.

> Almost all businesses have committed to transform themselves using these technological advances – at speed – and they are calling it Digital Transformation.

Ambition

If you talk to people working in leading/bleeding edge Digital projects, it is obvious that the ambition of these projects is unprecedented. The origin of these projects can be traced to some critical, but dateless assumptions being blown away. It's

---

[4] Internet.org is a Facebook-led organisation intending to bring the Internet to all humans on the planet.

easy to imagine some Digital expert convincing their client to do some blue-sky thinking for their latest and greatest project. "The rules of the game are changed" they might advise:

- There need be no human intervention in the interactions of your prospects and customers and your systems[5].

- Your sales and marketing messages can be created, sent to customers, followed up and changed almost instantly.

- You have the full range of data from the smallest locale to global in all media formats at your disposal.

- Autonomous drones, trucks and cars can transport products, materials and people.

- Physical products need not be ordered, held in stock and delivered at all – 3D printing might remove those constraints.

- And so on.

Systems of Systems and Ecosystems

According to NASA the Space Shuttle[6] - with 2.5 million parts and 230 miles of wire – is (or was) the most complex machine ever built by man. With about a billion parts, a Nimitz class supercarrier[7] is somewhat more complex. Of course, it comprises many, many machines that together comprise the super-complex system of systems – the modern aircraft carrier.

---

[5] Referred to as 'Autonomous Business Models'.

[6] http://spaceflight.nasa.gov/shuttle/upgrades/upgrades5.html

[7] http://science.howstuffworks.com/aircraft-carrier1.htm

A supercarrier has hundreds of thousands of interconnected systems and with its crew of 5-6,000 people could be compared to an average town afloat. Once at sea, the floating town is completely isolated except for its radio communications with base and other ships.

The supercarrier is comparable to what people are now calling Smart Cities. Wikipedia suggests this definition[8]:

"A smart city is an urban development vision to integrate multiple information and communication technology (ICT) and IoT solutions in a secure fashion to manage a city's assets – the city's assets include, but are not limited to, local departments' information systems, schools, libraries, transportation systems, hospitals, power plants, water supply networks, waste management, law enforcement, and other community services."

The systems of a Smart City might not be as complex as those of an aircraft carrier, but in terms of scale, the number of nodes and endpoints within the system might be anything from a million to billions.

A smart city is not just bigger than an aircraft carrier – it also has the potential to be far more complex. The inhabitants and many of the systems *move* in the realm of the city and beyond. They move and interact with each other in unpredictable ways. On top of that, the inhabitants are not hand-picked like the military; crooks, spies and terrorists can usually come and go as they please.

Unlike a ship – isolated at sea, the smart city is extremely vulnerable to attack from individuals and unfriendly governments and is comparatively unprepared for attack.

---

[8] https://en.wikipedia.org/wiki/Smart_city

But it's even more complicated than that.

Nowadays, every individual carries their own mobile system – a phone at least – with them. Every car, bus and truck might be connected. Some will be driverless. Every trash can, streetlight, office building, power point, network access point is a Machine to Machine (M2M) component of a Digital Ecosystem which has been defined thus:

"A Digital Ecosystem is a distributed, adaptive, open socio-technical system with properties of self-organisation, scalability and sustainability inspired from natural ecosystems"[9].

Systems of Every Scale

The picture I've been painting has probably given you the impression that the Digital systems being now architected and built are all of terrifying scale. But my real point is this: The scale of Digital ranges from the trivial to the largest systems mankind has ever attempted to build.

The simplest system might be, for example, a home automation product – where you can control the heating, lighting, TV and other devices using a console, your mobile phone or office PC. The number of components or nodes might be ten to thirty. A medium complexity system might be a factory automation, monitoring and management system where the number of components could be several thousand. The number of nodes in a Smart City will run into the millions.

The range of systems we now deal with spans a few dozen to millions of nodes. In the past, a super-complex system might have hundreds of interconnected servers. Today, systems are now connected using services or microservices – provided by

---

[9] https://en.wikipedia.org/wiki/Digital_ecosystem

servers. In the future, every node on a network – even simple sensors – is a server of some kind and there could be millions of them.

Systems with Social Impact

It might seem obvious to you now, but there is no avoiding the fact that Digital systems almost certainly have a social impact on a few, many or all citizens who encounter them. There are potentially huge consequences for us all as systems become more integrated with each other and with the fabric of society.

The scary notion of Big Brother[10] is set to become a reality – systems that monitor our every move, our buying, browsing and social activities – already exist. Deep or Machine Learning algorithms generate suggestions of what to buy, where to shop, who to meet, when to pay bills. They are designed to push notifications to us minute by minute.

Law enforcement will be a key user of CCTV, traffic, people and asset movement and our behaviours. Their goal might be to prevent crime by identifying suspicious behaviour and controlling the movement of law enforcement agents to places of high risk. But these systems have the potential to infringe our civil liberties too.

The legal frameworks of all nations embarking on Digital futures are some way behind the technology and the vision of a Digital Future that some governments are now forming.

---

[10] No, not the reality TV show. I mean the despotic leader of the totalitarian state, Oceania in George Orwell's terrifying vision, "1984".

In the democratic states, civil liberties and the rules of law are very closely monitored and protected. In non-democratic or rogue states, there may be no limit to what might be done.

Ecosystems of Ecosystems

The span of Digital covers commerce, agriculture, health, government, the media in its various forms and the military; it will affect the care, travel, logistics, and manufacturing industries. There isn't much that Digital won't affect in one way or another.

A systems view does not do it justice - it seems more appropriate to consider Digital systems as *ecosystems within ecosystems*.

The purpose of this book is to introduce the concept of Digital Assurance. The next chapter sets out what Assurance is.

2   What is Assurance?

In this chapter I want to touch upon some of the issues of conducting Assurance in real projects. If you are taking on an Assurance role, you should understand the different dynamic in which you must operate. Independent but accountable. It's a challenge, to say the least.

I'll use stories to illustrate some of the day to day challenges and make some recommendations for how you conduct yourself during what can be fraught periods.

Speaking Truth to Power

One of the key roles of Assurance is to articulate a meaningful message to the sponsors of the project you are engaged to oversee. The content, form and tone of that message are things you must figure out by agreement with your testing Stakeholders – in this case, a Project Board or steering group.

In one very large project I worked on, the Project Director – the person in charge of the entire development – briefed me like this.

"The Board meet every six weeks for a full day to review the status of the programme. The project team spend the whole morning setting out the status of the various projects that make up the programme. Your job is the make sure they aren't lying."

Over the six-week cycle, I attended meetings to review project status, decide on releases and transitions, reviewed plans, documents and exit reports and so on. At the Board meeting, the reports from the programme had to match what I had learned during the six weeks. On occasion, I intervened to explain technical points to the non-technical members of the Board, the risks of certain situations, the choices being offered and so on.

These sessions were highly detailed, candid and mostly informative.

Questions, Questions

Often you need to get informed on a project in a hurry. You also need to gather a ton of information from various sources from techies at the coalface to managers who may have little or no technical knowledge at all. You must be able to empathise with both and gain their trust – that you are there to help, not hinder.

If you want to know the type of questions to ask, I would refer you to The Tester's Pocketbook [1]. I am rather keen on models in testing, so as an example here is the summary of models and associated questions directly from the pocketbook.

Axiom: "Test Design is based on Models"

Choose test models to derive tests that are meaningful to Stakeholders. Recognise the models' limitations and the assumptions that the models make.

Consequence if ignored or violated

Tests design will be meaningless and not credible to Stakeholders.

Questions

- Are design models available to use as test models? Are they mandatory?

- What test models *could* be used to derive tests from the Test Basis?

- Which test models *will* be used?

- Are test models to be documented or are they purely mental models?

- What are the benefits of using these models?

- What simplifying assumptions do these models make?

- How will these models contribute to the delivery of evidence useful to the acceptance decision makers?

- How will these models combine to provide sufficient evidence without excessive duplication?

- How will the number of tests derived from models be bounded?

If you understand the core principles behind 'A New Model for Testing' [2] you are ready to help the rest of the business understand and visualise the business value chain. This will enable your team to collaborate effectively during the initial discovery and questioning phase and be capable of testing systematically, rather than instinctively.

The pocketbook presents sixteen Test Axioms – principles, if you like – and you can see a summary and all the questions for each at the Test Axioms website http://testaxioms.com.

First Advise, then Police

It is naïve to believe Assurance it just about testing; testing is only half the story. One of the benefits of a senior Assurance role is that you are involved early and can give independent advice in the earliest stages. I say on page 28 that *Assurance focuses on both the definition of a system and the testing of it*.

So, in the definition stage, you are looking to understand, for example:

- What are the sources of requirements knowledge?

- Who are responsible for communicating this to the project team?

- Are they the 'right' people, that is, responsible, knowledgeable and accountable to the business?

- Are the requirements 'trusted' before being used as the basis of development and testing?

- How do requirements transition from ideas to 'trusted'?

- How do requirements get captured? Is the format, granularity, language and tone fit for purpose?

- And so on.

So, what kind of advice might you offer to a project team? There are no bounds to the answer you get to your questions, and there is no formulaic answer I can offer you either.

Not very helpful, I hear you say.

Well, the challenge is that you must use your own knowledge and experience and the evidence presented to you to craft your suggestion to an individual or a team. The range of possibilities is rather too large to elaborate here, but a few examples should give you the idea.

The team takes feature requirements from a product owner and there is little discussion and thinking about estimated effort before they commit to coding. You might suggest they create some example scenarios that exercise the feature and walk through them with the product owner:

- *Are these scenarios consistent?*

- *Are there gaps in the requirement?*

- *Can outcomes be predicted for all inputs?*

Some years ago, I coined the mnemonic DeFOSPAM[11] for a method of challenging, validating and improving business stories.

The tester in the team spends a lot of time creating automated tests of new features via the user interface for the system. The goal is to build up the regression pack to protect the team from unwanted side-effects. Many of the test seem to be checking simple input validation functionality.

It looks like the tester is spending much more time getting automated scripts to work rather than creating and running effective tests. You might suggest:

- *The tester should work closer to developers and encourage them to create unit tests that validate user input in a more efficient way.*

- *The tester could design the tests and potentially write them on behalf of developers. Perhaps the developers integrate these tests into the CI service for the project.*

- *The tester spends less time on automation and more on exploratory, and in-depth tests of the user interface.*

The examples above are not 'rocket-science' and mostly reduce to some common-sense thinking.

To Improve, Focus on the Why, not the What

When trying to improve a situation, and offer suggestions for improvement, the critical Assurance activity is that you must

---

[11] If your team are using user or business stories you might find this blog post helpful: http://blog.gerrardconsulting.com/?q=node/604 It describes a method I called DeFOSPAM for challenging and improving story definitions.

not focus on what you believe is problematic behaviour. It is much more worthwhile to focus on <u>why</u> people behave a certain way.

> People adopt sub-optimal work practices because goals, conditions and attitudes – the context - make these practices workable. If you ask people to change their behaviour without changing the conditions they work in, they will always revert to their old behaviour when you leave them alone.

In the first example above, if the product owner has little time to spend with the team once they have shared their idea for a feature, it's unlikely the team will put effort into getting the requirement right. Their source of knowledge is absent – or not committed.

The product owner must show commitment to getting the definition right before you ask the team to challenge it.

In the second example, where the tester is doing all the automation, the problem might be that the developer feels it is not their responsibility and the tests thinks they are responsible for all testing. Naturally, the tester takes it upon themselves to get the Test Automation in place.

Testing happens at all stages in a development process. Developers should take ownership of Test Automation for tests that are appropriate at the unit level; testers should contribute to the definition of unit level tests (but not own them) to reduce the burden of less effective Test Automation at the UI level.

Automation

The major change in Digital projects from more traditional approaches (or Agile in most situations) is that there is a much greater focus on task automation. Obviously, Test Automation is a primary concern of the testers and Assurance. But pervasive automation brings its own unique challenges.

There are many and varied areas where automation comes to our aid. But there are risks at every stage and the role of Assurance is to identify these areas and ensure the tools are under the control of the team, and that the tools either:

- Base their automated decisions on appropriate evidence or
- Provide evidence in a timely and accessible format for humans to make decisions.

By evidence, I refer to the analytics output from tools that is used as the basis of decision-making.

The decisions to be made generally relate to the readiness of a process (often testing) to be performed or the adequacy of test outcome evidence that triggers an automated decision (to transition to another process or phase). The Assurance concerns are mostly related to things like:

- The readiness of an environment in terms of its configuration accuracy to host a system release
- The readiness of a release in terms of its build accuracy for testing or production use
- The readiness of tools to perform a test, capture results and provide evidence of completion
- The readiness of the tests themselves – are they in alignment with the version of the software to be tested?
- The coverage of tests being consistent with the goals of the test process itself
- The outcomes of the test, when analysed and interpreted lead to correct decision outcomes
- And so on.

It is likely that some of these require a detailed technical knowledge that you might not have. In your questioning, you will need to challenge the thinking behind the automation rather than the automation itself.

Experiment, Analytics and Assurance[12]

Obviously related to the notion of pervasive automation is the use of experimentation in production. The principle is clear – propose and make changes to a system, release it, monitor it, and based on the analytics decide what to do next. The change might be retained, rolled out to all users, withdrawn or persisted with to see if results get any better.

From the Assurance angle, you are interested in the nature of the experiment and how it will be measured. Typical experiments for an Ecommerce application would measure things like[13]:

- Page impressions, clicks or web service calls for a feature
- Product detail views
- Shopping cart updates
- Checkout steps and options chosen
- Transaction counts, response times
- Currency or localisation selections
- Coupon support, discounts and refunds etc.

---

[12] A great source book for this subject is [24]

[13] This list is partially derived from the Google Analytics support pages https://developers.google.com/analytics/solutions/ecommerce-platform

If the system is a website, then many of these measurements can be made by for example, Google Analytics, although there are many libraries now available to do this.

The measurements above focus on counting things, typically page or feature accesses or button clicks. But the time spent in a page or the elapsed time between events such as choosing a registration page and completing registrations might give you critical insights in where the delays and frustrations with your app lie.

It is now possible to track where on a mobile or browser screen a user clicks. From the stats collected by your application you can generate heat maps for a page which highlights where users touch and tap and where their time is spent. On mobile apps in particular, there are now logging apps that track all of the gestures your users apply when using your app. Clever stuff indeed.

How is the analytics data collected?

On a web page, embedded JavaScript might collect the data and post it to a logging server in an asynchronous way, so the user is not impeded by these messages. In native mobile apps 3rd party libraries designed to capture data log the data locally and post it periodically to some server for later analysis.

But it is quite common for app developers to write their own logging code that retains the data and does not share it with 3rd party services. Of course, the code (and data) is under your control, but you have the challenge of acquiring (or creating) your own data analysis subsystem somewhere along the line.

The immediate Assurance challenges here relate to the measurements and their relevance and meaning. Are they relevant? Are they meaningful?

But perhaps more importantly are the issues of privacy. Do your customers know, and are they comfortable that their browsing activity is logged and analysed? If you use 3rd party tools, is the data collection limited to what you specify? Or do these tools collect other data, not related to your immediate requirement?

Does the 3rd party analyse and profit from these analyses? Do they sell the results of analyses or do they sell private data to unknown parties?

There's Lots More of Concern

In the discussion above I have only touched on some of the issues that face Digital projects and where there is an Assurance concern. Here are some of the issues I haven't covered that are – to varying degrees – of concern.

User experience – perhaps the most important aspect of all. Measuring the user experience can partly be done by probes and logging user activity, and of course the allocation of scores to apps in an app store is of critical importance to the attractiveness of your app to new users.

Security – a discipline in its own right. The range of security-related risks grows every day – from penetration, listening, denial of service and so on. Increasingly, the targets for attack are the apps themselves. Hackers know that most application developers are not security experts and are relatively naïve in their designs – they are mostly untrained in 'secure coding'.

Device Characteristics – there are a growing number of characteristics and whose variation should be part of all test approaches for mobile devices. Hardware manufacturer, operating system and version, carrier, type of device, display size, multimedia capabilities, sensors (of which there might be 20), power supply/battery, connected hardware. All of these characteristics can be varied and are relevant to different classes of failure or vulnerability.

Cross-Platform Testing – there are many, many makes of devices and device types than can realistically be tested in a lab. For example, there are more than 24,000 different Android devices[14].

User-settings – all mobile devices offer their users a plethora of configuration options, many of which will affect the behaviour of your applications. How many significant settings are there for your app? Can you test them all? Is it worth the effort?

Performance – the most obvious challenge of a successful app is how it deals with rapid growth in its user base. The principles of performance management and testing are well known and the description in [3] from 2002 is still a reasonable overview of the subject (although the tools listing is out of date). Usually, performance tests of web service based architectures is straightforward. It is complexity of systems architectures in the cloud that sometimes make things a bit more difficult.

---

[14] http://opensignal.com/reports/2015/08/android-fragmentation/

3 Digital Assurance

Digital: Continuous Delivery

After that long introduction to the scale, potential complexity and societal risks of our Digital future in Chapter 1, and introducing Assurance in Chapter 2, we must now turn to what is the real subject of the book – Digital Assurance. The first chapter painted a huge canvas and daunting prospect. We now need to consider how businesses will acquire, build and assure Digital systems.

The headlong stampede to Digital and the transformations required have put more pressure than ever on IT systems development professionals. The business imperative is to take control of IT and change its culture from one of a brake on business to an accelerator.

This is not to say that IT has not been the foundation of some of the biggest and most successful companies on the planet. Rather, the use of IT has been limited by what IT can deliver in its traditional bureaucratic or piecemeal way.

Traditionally (and for most large organisations, currently) systems have been built using Waterfall or structured approaches (often described as V-Model[15]). The target solution is defined in great detail, and large programmes of work undertaken to deliver it. Almost all such projects overrun, and fail to deliver systems that meet the changed needs of business.

The Agile approach to systems development presumes that smaller, focused, motivated, autonomous teams can deliver

---

[15] https://en.wikipedia.org/wiki/V-Model

software faster. But large systems still need a lot of architecting and if this doesn't happen up front, then gluing diverse smaller systems later is still a painful process. Agile might scale technically, but at some point, the difficult task of integration must be performed. Agile can deliver quickly, but seems to be best suited to tactical programs, not strategic ones.[16]

The most successful Digital Transformation projects use what might be called Continuous or Adaptive approaches. These approaches use a blend of disciplines such as Continuous Delivery, DevOps, Shift-Left and the use of analytics or Shift-Right or Data-Driven Development.

This approach is not widespread yet, but the IT industry seems to have decided that this is the way forward with Digital – so it looks like it will slowly (or quickly in some organisations) supersede existing approaches based on some blend of structured and agile activities.

Continuous Delivery is regarded by many to be just an extension of what is commonly known as Agile. I don't think it is. There are significant differences between Structured and Agile as is well known. But there are differences again between Continuous and the other two approaches too.

To understand the difference between Structured, Agile and Continuous approaches, Table 1 lists the key attributes of the three approaches.

---

[16] Needless to say, there are many examples of successful and ongoing structured and agile development projects. I am generalising to make a broader point: Digital seems to work best using a third way.

Characteristic	Summary
Structure	What is the organisational structure of the project team?
Pace/cadence	What drives the rate of decision making? Who do decisions depend on?
Leadership	How is the team managed/directed? What style of leadership is involved?
Definition	How is requirements knowledge captured? In what format?
Testing	How is testing (mostly) performed? Scripted, exploratory, automated?
Automation	When is automation used? Who leads the automation effort?
Measurement	What/how is project measurement performed?
Governance	What form does governance take?

Table 1 Characteristics of development approaches.

Some of the differences are striking and I hope the narrative below makes it clear that we need to think differently if we move to a Continuous Delivery regime.

In Table 2 on the next page, the three approaches are compared side by side.

Characteristic	Structured	Agile	Continuous
Structure	Managed team	Autonomous	Production Cell
Pace/cadence	Business decision	Team decision	Feedback
Leadership	Project Managed	Guided Research	Line Managed
Definition	Fixed spec	Dynamic spec	Executable Specs
Testing	Scripted	Exploratory	Automated
Automation	Retrospective	Developer led	Pervasive
Measurement	Pervasive	Avoided	Analytics
Governance	Bureaucratic	Trust-based	Insight-Driven

Table 2 Comparison of the three development styles: Structured, Agile and Continuous

Organisational Structure – Production Cell[17]

In the continuous delivery paradigm, the team is most effectively organised as a production cell. Cells (sometimes called work cells) derive from lean manufacturing. Where a team create for example, large numbers of similar products, the most effective teams operate a 'flow' with minimal reference to (or interference from) people outside the team.

Software components are never identical but the process of scoping, estimation, development, test and deployment is repetitive in the context of different features. Cells work well – if they are autonomous and can rely on automated support.

Pace/Cadence – Feedback

The Scaled Agile Framework defines Cadence[18] as follows:

"Cadence and synchronization are the key constructs we use to build our Solution assets. **Cadence** is the use of a regular, predictive development rhythm. **Synchronization** causes multiple dependent events to happen at the same time."

The Cadence of a team is critical to delivery as the sequence of events to define, build, test and deploy are time boxed to fit into a regular, fixed cycle of delivery. The decisions to move from one phase to another e.g. from build to CI, to testing, to deployment are made based on feedback from the process – which is often automated.

---

[17] See e.g. http://www.strategosinc.com/cellular_manufacturing.htm

[18] "Develop on Cadence, Release Any Time", SAFE, http://www.scaledagileframework.com/develop-on-cadence-release-any-time/

Leadership – Line Managed

The production cell, flow and time boxed-activities depend on continuity, momentum, and a minimum of interruptions to the normal flow of work. In this respect, the management of a work cell is very like factory line management.

In comparison, projects are unique – they have specific deliverables, they are non-repetitive, they change the world in some way and have a start, a middle[19] and an end.

Definition – Executable Specifications

Whereas a traditional project sets out the solution requirement in a large document, in a Continuous Delivery team, the requirements are fed through the process in small well defined mini-specifications. Based on the well-established principle of Test Driven Development[20] and Behaviour-Driven Development[21], tests are used to define the behaviour of features before they are written. The goal is to automate the tests before the code is written and to retain those tests for the lifetime of the system (or at least feature). Hence the label, 'executable specifications'.

But it is well-known that the number of tests required to definitively specify behaviour is the same as that required to achieve exhaustive test coverage – infinite. So, tests must often be complemented by narrative descriptions or tabulated rules of behaviour to define the 'general case'.

---

[19] It's an old joke, but many projects have a start, a *muddle* and an end.

[20] https://en.wikipedia.org/wiki/Test-driven_development

[21] https://en.wikipedia.org/wiki/Behavior-driven_development

Testing – Automated

Now, if the tester is embedded in the work cell and works closely with the developer, they have very early visibility of the requirement and will typically discuss (as well as challenge) it with Stakeholders and developers. They will also see and have access to the software as it is written. So, it is natural for them to test informally, or in an exploratory manner whilst the paint is still wet, so to speak. In this way, the tester finds most bugs as early as is possible so they can be fixed promptly. This is the essence of the so-called Shift-Left approach – more of which later.

But as the developer deploys their code and unit tests to a CI regime, the tester might also add their own automated tests in parallel. These tests will tend to use the user interface and reflect user behaviour, rather than synthetic tests created by developers that are aimed at exercising specific aspects of code. At any rate, once the software leaves the developer and tester, all tests ought to be automated. There is little time left to manually test after that.

Automation - Pervasive

From the discussion of testing above, it's clear that the goal of the developer is to create all tests as automated – for all time. The testers might spend time doing exploratory testing in the period before the code is committed to CI but their goal also is to protect the project from unwanted side effects by creating a covering set of automated tests.

These tests will be based on a different model from developers (i.e. the user perspective) but they are designed not to exhaustively test, but rather act as a trip wire to detect regression failures. Automated tests are chosen specifically to cover critical, complex or error-prone areas of the software and to detect problems should a code change cause unwanted side-effects.

Overall, the goal is to automate all testing if possible.

Measurement - Analytics

In Chapter 8, I will define Test Analytics as:

"The capture, integration and analysis of test and production monitoring data to inform business and software development decision-making"

In Continuous Delivery, the lifecycle of all features includes deployment and release into production and monitoring, potentially for the lifetime of the feature. The purpose of monitoring and the analytics that follow is to assure that the feature is firstly, used, and secondly has the desired outcome or benefit. In many respects, feature developments are experiments – where the evidence of success or failure comes from analytics.

Governance – Insight-Driven

In such a dynamic environment, the notion of Governance, might be seen as an oxymoron. Governance is a big-business concern usually and the usual bureaucratic approach surely cannot work in a continuous delivery team. That is true, but the goals of governance are the same – it is the implementation that differs.

In a recent webinar, I presented a definition of governance [22]:

---

[22] http://blog.gerrardconsulting.com/?q=node/626

"Governance relates to decisions that define expectations, grant power or verify performance."

Assurance is 'Insight-Driven'. That same insight is consumed to drive continuous improvement.

Assurance

Drawing from the description of Governance above, and in the context of this book, the decisions that 'define expectations' and 'verify performance' are most relevant to the Assurance role. Although Assurance takes a holistic view on the organisation, process, people, tools and technologies used to create systems, most of our attention is focused on:

- Assuring the definition of a system and

- Assuring the testing, validation of that system.

These two goals – Assurance of the definition, requirement, specification, needs of a solution and the testing or validation of that solution drive all assurance activities. To achieve these goals, we need to be what I will label 'Stakeholder Obsessed'.

Stakeholder Obsessed

Testing is an information activity performed on behalf of (people who I call) testing Stakeholders. From the perspective of software testers, their Stakeholders tend to be their manager, end users or managers, developers or themselves (if they are a developer testing their own code).

Most systems that need testing have Stakeholders whose interests do not coincide perfectly. We cannot test everything, so we need to help them to make choices. We need to develop a good relationship with Stakeholders to build consensus, buy-in and trust in our test approach. Since most Stakeholders are non-technical, the language we use must be simple and direct. The Test Axioms defined in the Tester's Pocketbook [1] definitions are just that.

In the context of assurance, we are obsessed with the needs of these various Stakeholders, but our key Stakeholder, our sponsor in fact, should be the key decision maker or sponsor of the overall project. Only with this authority can we perform our assurance role.

Defining the Assurance Role

For the Assurance role to be effective, we need a crystal-clear definition of that role. This applies whether you work as an individual or have an assurance team. One way of defining this role for the benefit of our sponsor could be:

1. We operate with the authority of the chair or head of the project board[23], to whom we also report.
2. We have no responsibility for delivery – we are independent of the internal team or external suppliers or partners engaged in the project.
3. We are accountable for all assurance activities in the project. This includes all testing done by internal teams or suppliers or partners.

A decade or so ago, the three bullets above were my terms of reference for the assurance for of a 1000-man year, $200m software development programme. It seemed too terse to be meaningful, but it turned out to be extremely powerful.

---

[23] A project board is the most senior decision-making authority in a project. It might be called a management board or steering committee etc.

The first bullet – referencing our authority, conveyed from the chair of the project board gives us the power to ask any question, to obtain any evidence from the project participants. We are the representative of the project board. The proverb quoted at the start of the book, "Speak softly and carry a big stick…" is entirely relevant.

> You must operate with the authority of the project Stakeholders or you will not get the co-operation from the project team. Mention (but seldom use) your 'big stick' and you will go far.

Unless you are independent, you will have difficulty persuading the participants in the project to change their behaviour or to comply with your requests. Assurance makes people feel uncomfortable sometimes and they may force you to desist if you report to the same boss.

> Independence from the delivery and testing providers is essential to being objective and *to be seen as objective* by project Stakeholders.

The third bullet seems simple enough, but is quite subtle. Your assurance role is accountable for e.g. the testing on a project, but you are not responsible for performing it. How can this be achieved?

For all areas where you operate, your role typically has two phases. Initially you take an advisory role but after a while it morphs into a monitoring or even a policing role.

When you meet the project team initially they will brief you on their Test Strategy and process. In your advisory role, you might make some observations and recommendations. You should expect these to be acknowledged and implemented. You would advise that later on you will be checking for this and that the project board see your recommendations and later findings too.

When the time comes to monitor adherence to a strategy or process, you might review documents, attend and witness discussions and even be party to phase entry and exit decision meetings. Then, you will check that the process and your recommendations are being followed. Again, you will report to the project board.

> Your role has an early advisory phase and a later monitoring, policing phase. Your accountability requires that you exercise your authority to both advise and police.

That's a summary of the challenge and role of Assurance. The next five chapters discuss five key aspects of testing in Digital Projects: the use of models, Shift-Left, DevOps, the IoT and Shift-Right/Test Analytics.

4   Models at the heart of testing

Test Design is based on Models

In this chapter, I want to discuss the most important concept in testing – the art (or is it a science?) of creating and using models. Boris Beizer said in 1990 [4]:

> *'Testing is a process in which we create mental models of the environment, the program, human nature, and the tests themselves. Each model is used either until we accept the behaviour is correct or until the model is no longer sufficient for the purpose.'*

Test design is the process by which we select, from the infinite number possible, the tests that we believe will be most valuable to us and our Stakeholders. Our test model helps us to select tests in a systematic way. Test models are fundamental to testing and the rest of this chapter discusses their importance and use.

Fundamental Test Process

In the New Model for Testing [2] I suggest that, at the most fundamental level, all testing can be described thus:

1. We identify and explore Sources of Knowledge to build test models.
2. We use these models to challenge and validate the sources.
3. We use these models to inform (development and) testing.

I make a distinction between exploration and testing. The main difference from the common testing view is that I will use the term *Exploration* to mean the elicitation of knowledge about the system to be tested from *Sources of Knowledge*.

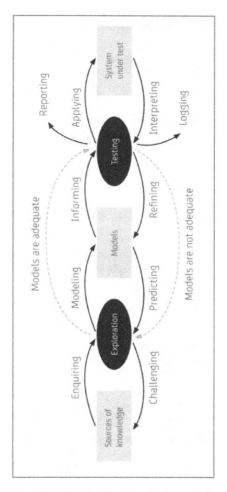

Figure 1 New Model Testing: Models at the heart of the tester's thinking processes.

Sources of Knowledge

We build our models from information that we elicit from Sources of Knowledge. Given a mission for testing, our first task is to identify these sources. These Sources of Knowledge might be:

- *Documentation:* specifications, designs, requirements, standards, guidelines and so on.
- *People:* Stakeholders, users, analysts, designers and developers and others.
- *Experience:* your own knowledge and experience of similar (or dissimilar systems), your preferences, prejudices, guesses, hunches, beliefs and biases.
- *System:* the system under test, if it exists, is available and is accessible.

We gather information from our Sources of Knowledge to derive models that we use to challenge our sources and design and/or test our systems.

All our Sources of Knowledge are fallible and incomplete and so are our models. Testers use experience, skill and judgement to sift through these sources, to compare and contrast them, to challenge them, to arrive at consensus. These capabilities are normally associated with systems or business analysts, of course.

What is a Test Model?

A test model might be a checklist or set of criteria; it could be a diagram derived from a design document or an analysis of narrative text. Many test models are never committed to paper – they can be mental models constructed specifically to guide the tester whilst they explore the system under test.

We use test models to:

- Simplify the context of the test. Irrelevant or negligible details are ignored in the model.
- Focus attention on one perspective of the behaviour of the system. These might be critical or risky features, technical aspects or user operations of interest, or aspects of the construction or architecture of the system.
- Generate a set of unique (within the context of the model) tests that are diverse (with respect to that model).
- Enable the testing to be estimated, planned, monitored and evaluated for its completeness (coverage).

From the tester's point of view, a model helps us to recognise aspects of the system that could be the subject of a test. The model focuses attention on areas of the system that are of interest.

An Example

Suppose we want to test how a car (an automatic gearshift model) accelerates from rest to its top speed and check that it meets our performance objective (e.g. from a standing start to 60 mph in 8 seconds). We might model this system as:

1. A mass (of the whole vehicle and driver) acting at a defined centre of gravity – which accelerates according to Newton's second law.
2. A power source (the engine) having a power output varying from a minimum to a maximum value dependent on the gas pedal position.
3. A gas pedal or accelerator that can have a variable position.
4. Formulae that relate the gas pedal position, power output and acceleration.

We can probably obtain all the information we need for our model from the design document for the car.

Using the model, we could design a test like this: "From rest, set the pedal to maximum power for a period of ten seconds. Use our formulae to calculate a predicted speed for every second of acceleration. Compare the actual speed with predicted speed every second of the test."

When we conduct the test in a real car we compare its speed at every second to that predicted by the model. In this way, we could determine whether the car meets its performance objective. For example, if the system under test (the car) does not reach the required speed at each measurement point in the test we either change the car, or we change the model (our interpretation of the car's design), or the design itself.

Everything looks fine – doesn't it?

Models Over-Simplify, So Use More Than One

But in the real test, our car may not behave as we expect because our model ignores several key aspects of the car's behaviour and context. We might reasonably ask:

- Would a real driver be as aggressive or gentler with the gas pedal?
- What is the wind speed and direction?
- What are the road conditions (wet, dry, tarmac, dirt, etc.)?
- What load is the car carrying, beyond the driver?
- Is the car on a level road, an uphill or downhill incline?

- What is the power efficiency of the system?[24]

Our model is grossly simplified, incorporates many implicit assumptions and would need significant refinement to be an accurate representation of a real car under test. *All models simplify the context of tests to varying extent,* so we normally use several models to broaden our view and coverage (referred to as 'diverse half-measures' [5]). The challenges are to select models that are an *accurate enough* representation of our system under test and to interpret the test outcomes obtained *with care.*

In general, all test models, even those proposed by textbooks, are heuristic in that they are useful in some situations but are always incomplete and fallible. Before we adopt a model, we need to know what aspects of the behaviour, design, modes of failure or usage patterns the model helps us to identify and what assumptions and simplifications it (explicitly or implicitly) includes.

Our Brains are Fantastic Modelling Engines

Our brains are capable of modelling and remodelling our surroundings. To achieve something as 'simple' as walking, our brain needs to understand, second by second (and faster than that) the configuration of the major bones in our body. It needs to understand the tensions in around one hundred muscles. To take a single step our brain needs to send impulses to all these muscles to work in highly complex patterns that enable us to move and reach our destinations without bumping into things. Our brain is simply not fast enough to process all this

---

[24] Even applying an efficiency rating would be a gross over-simplification. Typically, 80% of the power generated by burning gasoline is wasted heating the car and atmosphere, overcoming friction of car components, tyre wear and wind resistance.

information. It uses models to simplify and manage this challenge. Modelling and visualization are innate, essential skills required in all our everyday lives. The BEST robots on the planet are still quite crude in comparison.

You must have seen golfers practicing their swing before they take a shot. They rehearse and visualise the shot, the trajectory of the ball and the target. In many sports, coaches film athletes and talk them through their movements in detail helping them to visualise so they can control their movement, often under great physical stress. Athletes consciously model their world to achieve perfection or control and some call it 'the zone'.

But models don't only represent physical movement. For example, when Stephen Hawking lost physical capabilities, he invented a collection of powerful mental tools – models – that allowed him to carry on working with his physics, without using a blackboard or written formulae.

We use this same modelling skill to develop and test systems. Our brains are incredibly sophisticated and fast modelling engines and mental modelling dominates our thinking.

Models at the Heart of Testing

I suggest [2] that developer and tester exploration and modelling are quite similar. If testers are 'shifting left', pairing with developers or at least working more closely with developers, testers (and developers) need to be able to create models, learn how to articulate and share them and support better collaboration.

In a blog [6], "Courage and Ambition in Teaching and Learning", I suggest that the way we teach test design needs a rethink. Test design techniques are most often taught as clerical procedures. We need to teach testers how to create models, to appreciate them, to select them, and discard them. We need to teach the models that underpin the techniques, not just the procedures to implement them.

Thinking and modelling are at the heart of what testers do. The scale, complexity and rates of change in Digital Systems and the IoT are all on the rise. A new way of thinking and the acquisition and refinement of modelling skills must be our top priorities if we are to cope with these challenges.

5   Shift-Left

Background

Some five years ago, I coined the term 'redistributed testing' to describe a change in the testing business. Users, analysts, developers and testers would redistribute responsibility for testing and collaborate more effectively. The change would involve moving test activities (and possibly responsibilities) to the left and the term used for this approach is commonly called 'Shift-Left'.

Shift-Left can mean developers take more ownership and responsibility for their own testing; it can also mean testers get involved earlier, challenge requirements and feed examples through a Behaviour-Driven Development (BDD) process to developers. It can mean users and BAs together with developers take full responsibility for testing and it can mean no test team and no testers. We have seen all configurations and there is no 'one true way' of course.

Shift-Left is Not New

For as long as I've been in the testing business (1992) and certainly earlier than that, testing advocates have preached the mantra "test early, test often". The W-Model [7], introduced by my friend and colleague Paul Herzlich as long ago as 1993 suggested that all artefacts in a staged process – both documentary and software – can (and should often) be tested.

Although Waterfall was the dominant life-cycle approach at the time, the number or duration of stages are not what is important. The underlying principle was that *the Sources of Knowledge that provide direction for the design and development of software should be challenged or tested*. In a staged project, this might involve formal reviews. In an Agile project, the tester (or developer or BA or user) can suggest scenarios (examples) that challenge the author of a requirement or story to think-through concrete examples and discuss them before code is written.

Shift-Left is mostly about bringing the thinking about testing earlier in the process.

So, all that Shift-Left requires is that the testers get involved earlier and ask awkward questions? Is it really as simple as that? Well, not quite.

What is Driving Shift-Left?

Several changes in the market are at play and are driving new behaviours in our industry. Some started around five years ago but others are more recent. But what is meant by 'started'? Started means there were enough people promoting new approaches that showed evidence of success and were sufficiently credible for others to adopt them. These approaches 'crossed the chasm' as Geoffrey Moore describes it [8], and became viable for the wider business and IT community.

These are the main changes involved in the shift-left phenomena:

1. The Behaviour Driven Development (BDD) approach has allowed developers, users/BAs and testers to engage around what might be called business stories. Test-Driven Development has been used by many, but not all, developers for 15 or more years. BDD is being adopted more widely as it encourages better collaboration in Agile teams as well as introducing tools that can be used by developers less onerous Test-First approach.
2. The concept of Continuous Delivery (CD) [9], again, has been around for 5-10 years and its roots are in the highly

automated build and release automation approaches pioneered by large online businesses. It is now adopted by most organisations with an online presence.

3. CD systematised and accelerated the release process through automation. But it then highlighted the delays in production deployment and infrastructure change that had previously been masked by slow build, test and release processes. DevOps is a cultural and mind-set change whereby developers collaborate much more closely with operations staff. Right now, new tools appear almost daily and vendors promote DevOps as the 'next big thing'. It is a very hyped and dynamic situation.

4. SMAC, or Social, Mobile, Analytics and Cloud represents a shift in the way organisations are managing business and systems' change in the mobile space. Experimentation in business, implemented as production systems changes, are monitored at a detailed level. The "Big" data captured is processed and business decisions are made based on the analytics obtained.

Frequent experimentation with production systems enables business innovation 'at the speed of marketing'. Experimentation is at the heart of what seems to be the most important bandwagon of the 2010s – Digital Transformation'. Digital Transformation or just 'Digital', is getting most of the attention (and budget) right now. Marketers are promising faster and better access to consumers through more channels – mostly mobile.

My paper 'Digital Transformation, Testing and Automation' [10] describes the Digital revolution and proposes some responses, so might be of interest.

What Does Shift-Left Mean to Testers?

Shift-Left implies that whenever it is possible to provide feedback that will help the team to understand, challenge and improve, goals, requirements, design or implementation – that feedback should be provided. This behaviour comes as second-nature to many, but not all, testers. Users, BAs, developers and the entire team should be ready to both provide and accept feedback in this way. There might be resistance, but the overall aim is to run a better, more informed project – that's all.

What does the tester do in the shift-left world of testing? Well, the easiest way to summarise this behaviour is, 'get involved early' – as early as possible. Engage in the discussion and collaborate on ideas, requirements and every stage where the outcome of that stage has a bearing on the value of the final deliverable of the project. Put simply, the tester challenges Sources of Knowledge, whether these sources are Stakeholders, users, developers, business stories, documents or received wisdom.

The most common approach is to 'challenge through example'. At all stages, these examples can be regarded as tests. They might be discarded quickly after use, or be codified into Test Automation or manual checks. These examples could just be used tactically to point out flaws in peoples' thinking, or be provided to developers, say, as ideas or seeds for developer tests. They might also be used as a coaching aid to help users or developers to see how better tests can be created.

Software projects have been described as a knowledge acquisition process [11]. This knowledge is gathered throughout the project and often evolves over time. The goal of shift-left is to assure this knowledge through challenge and testing close to its source and to ensure, where possible, that it is trusted before it is frozen in code.

Shift-Left takes the Test-First philosophy further. Agile has always promoted collaboration and rapid feedback and Shift-Left could be viewed, simply, as the ultimate rapid-feedback approach.

If you adopt it, Shift-Left has a profound effect on how you work as a tester.

As a Tester, how do I Apply Shift-Left?

It looks like Shift-Left is not just a fad, and it's coming your way. How will it affect you if you work in a system test team? If you are part of an Agile Team, does it still matter? What should you do?

We have advocated the Shift-Left approach as core to Test Strategy in Agile projects for some time. In an Agile context, Test Strategy can be viewed as a series of 'Agile Interventions'. There are critical moments in all projects where opportunities to gather and present feedback present themselves. The tester needs to focus on these critical moments and be ready to contribute at those times.

I presented the thinking behind this approach in a recent webinar [12] and I use a client case study to illustrate where these interventions might occur. In your own projects, you need to identify your 'critical moments', and identify the choices that you and your team can make. For example, should you write unit tests for developers, provide examples to get them started or should you coach them to improve their testing ability?

Your role will almost certainly change. It may be that testers, not just thinking, are shifted left and you become the testing servant of developers. This probably is not the best outcome for you or your project. We suggest you identify the critical moments, propose your contribution and negotiate with your team. You offer more test leadership and guidance rather than volunteering simply to take on responsibility for the testing work. It will be much easier to demonstrate your value to the team if you take this approach – the team won't need as many testers.

I'm a Test Lead/Manager. What Should I Do?

If you are a test manager or a test lead now, it might be harder to justify your role if the intent of management is to reduce the cost of testing by shifting left. If your organisation is moving in this direction, you probably have a longer-term career decision to make. Where do you want to be in five years? In six months? We have identified five broad choices that might be open to you.

1. Providing test and assurance skills to business: moving up the food chain towards your Stakeholders, your role could be to provide advice to business leaders wishing to take control of their IT projects. As an independent agent, you understand business concerns and communicate them to projects. You advise and cajole project leadership, review their performance and achievement and interpret outputs and advise your Stakeholders.
2. Managing Requirements knowledge: In this role, you take control of the knowledge required to define and build systems. Using your critical skills, you ensure clarity and precision in requirements and the examples that illustrate features in use. You help business and developers to decide when requirements can be trusted to the degree that software can reasonably be built and tested. You manage the requirements and glossary and dictionary of usage of business concepts and data items. You provide a business impact analysis service.
3. Be a TestMaster – providing an assurance function to teams, projects and Stakeholders: A similar role to 1 above – but for more Agile-oriented environments. You are a specialist test and assurance practitioner that keeps Agile

projects honest. You work closely with on-site customers and product owners. You help projects to recognise and react to risk, coach and mentor the team and manage their testing activities and on occasion, do some testing too.

4.	Be a DevOpsMaster – managing the critical information flow to and from DevOps processes (automated build, test and deployment processes). This information flow is critical. Perhaps you could define and oversee the processes used to manage the flows that enable control of change, testing and delivery.

5.	Managing outsourced/offshore teams: In this case, you relinquish your onsite test team and manage the transfer of work to outsourced or offshore suppliers. You are expert in the information flow and manage the relationship with the outsourced test team, monitor their performance and assure the outputs from them.

If you haven't been shifted left yet, then you should look around both inside and outside your team and think about how your role might change soon. Your role will eventually change, but you should have some choice of how it evolves. I wish you luck in your choices.

6   DevOps

Background

I want now to discuss the adoption of DevOps from a tester and testing perspective. The DevOps movement (for want of a better label) is progressing rapidly. Like many other moves the industry has made, the speed of adoption accelerates faster than the definition of the movement itself. DevOps is still not well defined and the nuances of culture, the emergent capability of new technologies and range of (mostly successful) case studies means the issues at hand are still widely debated [13].

Depending on who you talk to, DevOps can be a solution to a problem or a goal in itself. In some businesses, the goal is 'Going Digital' and DevOps is part of the overall approach to delivering frequently and with high quality. This is the context I'll assume in this paper. But in the marketing of DevOps-related technologies and services, this goal can be obscured. The challenge of the cultural change (or more concretely, behaviour change) required for success is frequently underestimated.

The other assumption I'll make is that the testers involved in and affected by DevOps are new to the whole idea. I'll shape this chapter as an introduction to DevOps for these testers as well as a discussion of its impact on test practices. If you are an experienced DevOps practitioner, I hope you still find the chapter useful. If you are not a tester, you will at least see the tester's perspective.

For the Uninitiated: What is DevOps?

Simplistically, DevOps is a label put on the notion of Development and Systems Operations teams working more closely. In the so-called Delivery Pipeline, from source code commit to operation in production, Developers accommodate and automate some of Operations activities. Operations have more visibility of and some influence over the activities of Developers. The motivation for this is primarily to speed up the deployment and implementation of software. Bringing Ops and Dev closer together – effectively into an Agile team – implements what might be called 'Agile Operations'.

The most obvious outcome of successful DevOps implementations is the reduction in the time it takes for software changes to transition from an idea to production operation. When a developer says a software change is 'done', the transition to production usage is performed with the aid of pervasive automation. Automated tools and processes are used in system configuration, the build process, in testing, the deployment to test, staging and production environments, in post-deployment monitoring, in evaluation and in operation.

So, DevOps is just about tools then?

At one level, the goal of DevOps is to eliminate bottlenecks in the delivery pipeline through automation. But automation of staged processes still require governance. Most automated processes are not autonomous – they cannot complete their tasks without human intervention in maintenance or in handling exceptions. A fully automated DevOps process is meaningless without consideration of the human factor. Although tools do a lot of heavy-lifting, it is the people running the process that make it work – or fail.

So, DevOps is just Dev and Ops people working more closely with the aid of tools then?

No, it's not that either. The handoffs between automated processes often involve other processes – usually testing of one kind or another. Automated tests need to be created by Developers and Testers. The output of these tests is focused on providing sufficient information for other processes, or, just as often, people, to transition between stages in the pipeline. Testers, and Developers who test, provide the assurance that the DevOps process delivers successfully and reliably.

'My head hurts, what is DevOps really?' I must say, it's an evolving, emergent discipline. The question is posed and discussed at length in an excellent post here [13]. The definition of DevOps is still not settled. Perhaps it never will be.

What does that mean for testers? It means that there is still not 'one true way' and that your role in a DevOps regime that is evolving (and every regime is evolving) is not yet fixed. There are two main contributions you can make:

1. You need to pay attention to the things that hurt and work to make them less painful.

2. You need to identify the opportunities and interventions that will add value to the DevOps process.

If there is one mantra that best describes the driver towards DevOps it is 'if it hurts, do it more'. It might be a bit of a cliché, but I'll use that as the context for implementing and improving DevOps test practices.

If it Hurts, Do it More (Often)

The difficulty or pain we experience when doing some tasks influences us adversely. If we don't like to do a task, we tend to put it off. When we finally take the task on – it is more painful. Visiting the dentist, cleaning the garage, integrating software, testing and so on. Our experience is commonly that the less frequently we perform these tasks the more traumatic the task is when we do it. Martin Fowler [14] suggests three reasons why frequent or even continuous execution of certain tasks reduces the pain.

The first is that larger, more complex tasks are hard to plan, manage and control – breaking up large tasks makes them easier to do, less risky and if something does go wrong, easier to unwind. The second is that many tasks (and testing is the shining example) provide feedback. That feedback, if received early and often, means that problems can be addressed rapidly and certainly before any further time is wasted. Thirdly, if we practice an activity more frequently – we get better at it. We learn how to do it efficiently. We may also see opportunities to automate it in some way.

From the tester's perspective, this mantra forces us to take much more seriously the notion of automation in the testing process. If there are manual interventions (typically between automated stages in the DevOps process) these will be seen to be the pain points – the bottlenecks, the causes of delays, and the potentially less reliable and error-prone aspects of the process. Manual testing is painful. Yes, you might love exploratory testing, you might fear that only you, as a human, can find those gnarly bugs that automation will never find, that you as the tester are the only person trustworthy to prevent disaster happening.

It might be painful for you, as a tester, to trust developers and automation to do the testing job properly. If it hurts, you must do it more often.

Tests, Automation and Trust

There is much debate around the meaning of, for example, checking and testing [15], and the reliance we can place on testers, on checks and automation [1, 6].

I am not saying we can place all our faith in automated checks. We certainly need more sophistication than that. But we can, for our current purpose, at least separate tests and test execution activity into four components.

1. Checks that can be automated by developers as part of their component-level check-in and Continuous Integration (CI) processes.

2. Checks that can be automated (typically by system testers) to exercise API-level, link or end-to-end transactions.

3. Tests that can perform compatibility checks to demonstrate compatibility across browsers, operating systems, platforms.

4. Tests that can only be performed by a human.

I can only offer a few suggestions on how to make these distinctions – every environment is different, of course. The more germane question for now is, "How does the tester 'let go' of late, manual checking?" I have talked about the elimination of late, manual checking before [17]. It requires proactive effort and trust.

These will be the focus of your efforts:

1. Wherever possible, manual checks that could be performed at a component level should be pushed forward to the developers. As a tester, you might suggest these tests in a pairing or whiteboard session. You might have to write them yourself and include them in the CI regime.

2. End-to-end or user interface tests may require automation. These need to be minimized, as they tend to be slow to run, brittle and frequently require maintenance. Consider whether they need to be run at every code check-in, or could be reserved for use on larger, less frequent releases only.

3. What manual-only tests could be run on components that are not yet integrated into a release candidate?

Can the manual testing be performed in pairing sessions with developers? Are there alternatives to this testing? Could story-boarding, BDD-style prototyping help? Could UI checks be performed on mock-ups or wire-frames?

4. Which checks need only be run once, manually, as opposed to checks that need to be retained for regression purposes – and are candidates for automation?

I mentioned the notion of trust above. Another way of looking at this is to speculate on how a system could be reliably tested if there were no late manual testing at all. Imagine an environment where all the testing was done by tools. Would your concerns be dominated by the fact that you simply don't trust the developers to do a good job of testing? Moving testing thinking to the left (as suggested in the last chapter) should reduce the doubt. If, as a tester, you act more as a pathfinder – to identify risks and assess them, to select tests and ensure that they are incorporated into the development and automation, your concerns could be minimized.

Certainly, you must stop believing you are the gatekeeper of quality, the last defense, the only person who cares. You must think more like a visionary, risk-identifier, risk manager, pathfinder, a facilitator and a coach/mentor.

Practice, Monitoring and Improvement

With all the good intentions of reducing or eliminating reliance on late manual checking, bugs will still get through. When software is released into production, problems arise. One of the key disciplines of DevOps from the operations point of view is a deeper level of monitoring.

Monitoring at every layer, from components and simple transactions in the applications, through integration and messaging and of course the infrastructure itself. One goal of monitoring is to raise alerts on failure before users experience the impact of them. This is rather ambitious, but this is the ultimate goal.

When problems are encountered in production, the task then is to use the analytics derived from monitoring to not only trace the cause and resolve it, but also to refine the test process, automated or manual, to reduce the likelihood of similar problems in the future. The role of testing and analytics across the entire pipeline process was introduced and discussed here [18].

One could call the automated tests in the DevOps process 'monitoring'. Coupled with monitoring in production one could say that monitoring throughout the DevOps process and into production enlarges the scope of testing. DevOps, therefore, does not diminish the role of testers.

Conclusion

I was recently asked *'When should DevOps not be attempted in an organisation?'* It's a good question but I think what's behind it is concern over whether DevOps is here to stay and whether testers should take notice? My answer is simple.

Why wouldn't you want developers and operations people talking to each other? Why wouldn't you want more reliable builds and deployments into test and production? Why wouldn't you want the best of technology to support more accurate, efficient and informative pipelines?

DevOps is a good thing but not always easy to achieve – it requires cultural change and that isn't always easy.

For the tester, DevOps gives us greater influence in the early stages of projects, forces us to think more seriously about automation in testing, information provision and decision-making. Testers need to embrace DevOps because it provides opportunities to be pro-active, gain more authority and respect in our project teams.

7   Internet of Things (IoT)

Introduction

In this chapter, I'll explore how the IoT – also known as the Internet of Everything (IoE) – will affect testing and testers.

It seems like everything will become 'smart' eventually. In parallel with domestic applications, industries such as retail, manufacturing, transport, agriculture and telecommunications are embracing the IoT with enthusiasm. Needless to say, Government and the military are pressing on with research and, of course, the emerging phenomena – smart cities – will watch over or control our daily lives.

This chapter references a series of articles I have written [19, 20, 21] and draws some conclusions on the impact on testing and testers.

A Layered Model of the IoE

In the same way that standards for networking devices at the periphery are evolving, there is no standard or conventional architecture for the IoE. However, some patterns are emerging and, as might be expected, the architecture can be split into logical layers.

This seven-layer model is an amalgam of several styles of schematic that have been published. This one is device and product neutral and it is not aligned with any technology. In terms of scale and perspective, these layers look best drawn as a hierarchy with the device layer at the base.

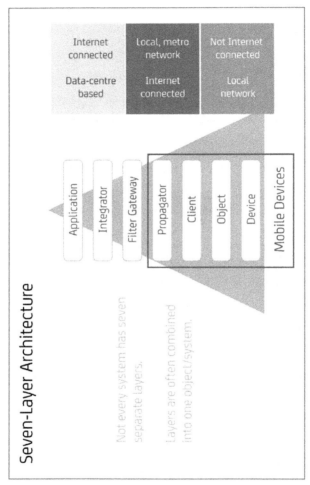

Figure 2 Seven-Layer Architecture of the IoT

The seven layers are described in [20]. Regardless of implementation, the layered model should help you to understand the architecture of your system.

The Risks of Failure

The seven-layer architecture might help you to understand the function of each component in an IoE implementation. I've used the layered model to create a list of what I would call risk patterns [20].

But there are also societal or personal risks that are being aired in the media and that we need to pay some attention to. These may or may not exist for your application – but if they do, they are likely to be unique to your project. Here are the main contenders:

- Social/Personal Risks: Security and privacy dominate.
- Complexity: Interactions between devices may be unpredicted, unforeseen and unknown.
- Privacy: Data collection is pervasive but invisible and largely out of our control.
- Abuse: The IoT brings benefits, but the pervasiveness of networks and data invites criminal activity.
- Corporate Security: Previously secure company systems are now being connected to much larger, insecure networks.

In contexts such as transportation systems, manufacturing production lines, TV stations, energy generation/distribution and smart cities, the potential for hacking, disruption and terrorism is unbounded. The security industry has a lot to learn and more to do. The IoT is a whole new ball game.

The IoE brings new levels of complexity and scale. The non-functional risks are reasonably well-known and we know how to address them. *What is new is the need to do functional testing and simulation at scale.*

The Scope of IoE Testing

The range of concerns that the IoE brings is wider than ever before. Not all IoT systems will be huge, complex and expensive but all provide a different technical and risk profile than we are used to. Here are the main dimensions of scope for the IoT Tester:

- Hardware-Level testing: the lowest level devices are sophisticated, but perform simple functions. Most will be performed by manufacturers.
- Scale: a wearable application might be simple in its architecture, but could be scaled to a user-base of millions.
- Object and Server level functionality: Most functional testing will take place at the level of local hubs, aggregators and data-centre-based servers. Architectures will range from simple web-apps to systems with dozens of sub-systems.
- Mobile objects: These move in and out of the range of networks and roam across networks. Environmental conditions, the sources of data and device location affect behaviour. Power, interference, network strength, roaming and jamming issues will all have an effect.
- Moving networks: Some systems (e.g. connected cars) carry their own local network. A network that moves will encounter other networks that interfere

or may introduce a rogue or insecure network into range and pose security problems.

- Network security risks are at many levels: Rogue devices use your network and eavesdrop or inject fake data. Rogue access points hijack your users' connections and data. Vulnerabilities exist at all levels in your architecture and are prone to attack.
- Device registration, provisioning, failure and security: Initial device registration and provisioning are failure-prone. Devices are prone to power failures, snow, heat, cold, vandals, animals, thieves and so on. Power-down, power-up and automated authentication, configuration and registration processes may need to be tested.
- Collaboration confusion: Moving devices (e.g. cars, again) collaborate in complex ways and in large numbers. But accidents happen, drivers change their mind, car park spaces will become available and unavailable randomly and so the optimisation algorithm must cope with rapidly changing situations. At the same time, these services must not confuse users.
- Integration at every level: Simple and complex flows of data and control – end to end.
- Big Data – logistics: Substantial data storage services will be part of the system to be tested.
- Big-Data – Analysis and visualization: Data science and visualization are likely to be in the scope of the IoT. This includes timely, accurate and consistent data as well as filtering, merging, integration, and reconciliations too.

- Personal and corporate privacy: Hackers and crooks are one threat, but your own Government may be seen to be another potential villain.
- Wearables and embedded: Wearable and human-embedded devices provide new and unique challenges.
- Everything connected: The time will come when all the devices used in a hospital, hotels and factory for example will be connected.

The range of issues we need to consider in testing the IoE has increased and the scale of the testing required has increased too.

Functional Testing at Scale

When we test the functionality of components higher in the architecture, particularly the integrator and application level, we might have to simulate thousands or millions of devices in the field. The numbers of combinations and permutations may be beyond computation or prediction. Our simulations will repeatedly generate scenarios to be tested, record the outcomes and might replay the simulations for later study.

The higher-level components must be testable. We'll need facilities like exception handlers, utilities that inject data, capture and reproduce or replay scenarios. Cem Kaner has written quite a lot about what he calls 'High Volume Automated Testing' [22]. This is a good starting point.

These techniques could also be called Big Data testing. We'll need to find data that fits our purpose; we'll need to generate, tag, edit and seed data so we can trace its usage; we'll need tools to monitor the use of tagged data and the ability to reconcile data from collection, storage, use and disposal. We'll need new test visualization tools to support diagnostics and debugging.

This is a volumes game. Individual tests may or may not be important, but we'll spend a lot of time dealing with large scale outcomes, visualizations and decision-making.

Test Environments; Testing in the Field

In a simple case, a test lab for a home environment management product could be set up in any office as the scope of the local network is confined to a single household. In the case of an urban environmental management system that monitors air pollution levels across a city, for example, the sensor data capture could be simulated in a lab. However, we would expect to have to pilot the service in a real city environment to calibrate the sensors, data aggregation and integration processes to obtain meaningful data visualizations.

Tool Support

Although there will always be a need and opportunity to do manual testing, a much larger proportion of testing must be performed by tools than we are currently used to. The tools will need to execute very large numbers of tests. The challenge is not that we need tools to execute tests. *The challenge will be, "how do we design the hundreds, thousands or millions of tests that we need to feed the tools?"*

The devices now appearing all have their nuances and complications and will experience unexpected events. Even a simple system could encounter thousands of scenarios. Systems are getting more complex and these need testing. It's only going one way.

Test Analytics, Visualization and Decision-Making

I will expand on Test Analytics later. If your production systems are platforms for experimentation, then the code that serves marketers can also serve developers and testers. Think of your analytics code as your sensor network. DevOps processes are things, too.

Performance Testing and Test Data

Performance testing in an IoT world is not much different from our current experience. What may make life harder is when the data that is captured by sensors must be coherent. For example, the messages received from cars in a city must match a physical location to be meaningful. A randomly generated set of location co-ordinates will not do. We'll need trusted data sets from real world operation or utilities that can generate meaningful and trustworthy data for testing.

The Future for Testing and Testers

It seems to me that high levels of Test Automation are bound to be required to make the IoE a reality. *Automation will not make testing easy; it will make testing possible.*

Test Automation in a DevOps environment is a source of data for analysis just like production systems so analysis techniques and tools are another growing area.

Should testers learn how to write code? I have a simple answer – yes. Now it is possible that your job does not require it. But the trend in the US and Europe is for job ads to specify coding skills and other technical capabilities. More and more, you will be required to write your own utilities, download, configure and adapt open source tools or create automated tests.

The IoT and Digital trends are pushing testing to the left. It seems like every company is pursuing what is commonly called a 'Shift-Left' approach. The activities, or rather, the *thinking activities* of testing are being moved earlier in the development process. My advice is – embrace it.

Summary

The IoT increases testing in scale, diversity and complexity.

Testing low-level components or sub-system testing is pretty much the same as before. But at the system level, we'll need simulation methods and high volume Test Automation. The tools we need may not yet exist so you may have to create your own, until the tools suppliers catch up.

High volume Test Automation requires test models, test data generators and automatic oracles. Modelling, simulation, analytics, visualization and tool-supported decision-making will become important capabilities of test architects and testing teams. Testers must learn how to create better test models and how to use them with more technical modelling and simulation tools.

Creating trustworthy test environments and meaningful test data will cause big headaches (as always).

Large-scale test environments in the lab and environments in the field will be required and the boundaries between experimentation in production and testing in the lab will become blurred. Test analytics derived from DevOps processes will become a critical discipline in testing the IoT.

8 Testing, Analytics and Decision-Making (Shift-Right)

Introduction

At the most fundamental level, the purpose of testing is to gather information to learn about some aspect of a system and make a decision based on the outcome of one or more tests [1]. Testing provides the most valuable information required by developers (to fix defects), project managers (to understand and manage progress) and Stakeholders (to be updated and assured). In this one respect, testing is all-powerful – it is the single source of knowledge of achievement in systems projects.

In the Digital or Mobile space, businesses are releasing apps that capture information about their users and the usage patterns of their apps themselves. Every app nowadays collects data in real time and sends it back to the provider in more or less real time too. This data is analyzed to detect trends, patterns of behaviour, user preferences and opportunities for improvement or new market initiatives. The apps are instrumented to collect information for decision making.

Introducing Test Analytics

In my paper, Thinking Big, Introducing Test Analytics [23], I make the case for looking at pre-release testing and production monitoring and analytics after release as two activities in a continuum. I use the term Test Analytics as the label for a discipline that spans the entire lifecycle from idea through development, production and eventual retirement. A comprehensive review of mobile testing and analytics can be found in The Mobile Analytics Playbook [24].

I define Test Analytics as:

"The capture, integration and analysis of test and production monitoring data to inform business and software development decision-making"

Usually, testers have treated the output from test management tools as the main source of information for reporting. But this is far too limited a viewpoint. Counts of test cases, requirements covered (whatever that means), incident or bug reports raised, triaged, fixed or ignored summarized and in time series are interesting, but limiting too.

Modern Practices – Opportunities for Testing

Earlier chapters shed some light on how we can improve our reporting and analyses. The thinking behind Shift-Left, test models, DevOps and automation and the emerging testing disciplines they encourage are forcing us to rethink what we mean by test reporting. The fundamental goal of testing – to collect and analyze data to inform decision-making – is unchanged, but there are many opportunities for improving the way we report from testing:

1. The Shift-Left discipline aims to reduce, if not eliminate, misunderstandings in requirements early on. Late, costly requirements defects and crises will not confuse our reporting.

2. The move to pervasive automation in DevOps regimes generates much of the data we need automatically. Results capture and analyses are no longer manual; reporting is almost instant.

3. The New Model for Testing [1] puts modelling at the heart of test design. When testers use meaningful models, they enable more meaningful coverage measurement.

4. Test Analytics can also be captured during exploratory sessions. Usage and system models can be created before test sessions as charters, while test coverage during sessions can be captured in-flight.

5. Testing in production is increasingly common. Why? No one can test all mobile device types (there are more than 24,000 Android devices 'out there' [25]). The value of production monitoring analytics is clear.

6. Monitoring, logging, alerting and analytics products are more widely available. Applications are instrumented as well as infrastructure. Scenarios that testers couldn't try in the lab can be monitored (tested) in the field.

7. Some companies are abandoning bureaucratic incident management procedures. When defects are found – they are fixed without debate or delay.

8. Incidents are gone. The source code control tool, the automated unit tests that drive and protect change provide the evidence and new visualizations of change and impact. See [26] for an example of what is possible.

Because of these new practices, techniques, tools and visualizations, the nature of testing is changing. We have a real opportunity to improve our core product – the information we provide to Stakeholders. But how does testing support decision-making?

Testing and Decision-Making

I've been involved in many testing projects, large and small over the years. In each one, the inevitable moment of decision comes at the end of a phase of testing – what do we do next? Do we release to the next phase? Do we release to production or customers? Do we delay and extend the project? Do we pause and re-think our goals? Do we abandon hope and kill the project?

These are all critical sounding decisions, but decisions are made at many levels. For example, when a tester finds a problem and discusses it with a user and the developer. The decisions come quickly: Is it a bug? Can it be fixed? Can it be fixed quickly? What is the impact of change? Is there a viable workaround? Is it worth fixing? Does the problem matter to the user at all?

Testing supports decision making at all levels. Testing Stakeholders (executives, customers, users, project managers, operations, and developers) can have many roles. So, the information they require from testing varies in line with their perspective and their need to make decisions. There is no magic formula for deciding what information is required – we must ask our Stakeholders what they would find most useful, valuable and economic.

But there's a problem. How can we quantify testing? It's easy enough to count the cost, but how much testing is enough? What is the value of testing anyway? These are difficult questions that testers must answer.

I am a big fan of physics and as a bit of fun, I have used some scientific-sounding labels to name one testing principle and two testing theories.

The Testing Uncertainty Principle

If you have ever planned to do 'enough testing' (whatever that means) and predict a completion date for the testing, you will recall how hard it is to derive a reliable estimate. If you expect to find problems (and who doesn't?), the biggest test planning questions are 'by how much will testing be delayed?' and 'how much re-testing will be required?' the answers depend mostly on how many bugs you encounter and how hard they are to fix and test. But you will never know this until the bulk of your testing, and fixing and re-testing are complete. It's yet another testing paradox.

The challenge of test prediction and planning is conveniently expressed in the *Testing Uncertainty Principle*:

▪ *We can predict test status, but not when it will be achieved;*

▪ *We can predict when a test will end, but not its status.*

You can define an exit or completion criteria – 'all tests run and passed' – but you can never be sure when you'll reach that point – until you reach it. How often do we set exit criteria and fail to meet them? We have to treat exit criteria as planning assumptions. If we don't meet the criteria, our assumptions are wrong, our plan is wrong and we need to re-plan, or re-scope the project.

We can time-box the testing and guarantee a finish date. But who knows how much testing we can fit into the period and whether that is enough?

The Testing Theory of Relativity

The value of a test is affected by many things. A single test case might cover five lines of code in a component unit test. Another might exercise five million lines of code in a large system.

Clearly the second test has more value. But who can say what that value is?

We must ask a less ambitious question. The tester might have a view, but we must rely on our Stakeholders to judge value. They cannot put a value on any test – but they can usually say which of two or more tests is the most valuable. In this respect, we cannot assign an absolute value, but we can discern a relative value – one test is more or less valuable than another. This sounds like a big disadvantage – but it isn't really.

Most of the challenge of test planning comes down to scope. We know we cannot test everything so we must prioritise in some way. Knowing the relative value of tests means we should be able to select the more valuable ones and set the other less valuable tests aside – for now.

Only the Stakeholder(s) we test on behalf of can judge the value of tests.

But wait a minute – what about the risks of failure? Isn't the value of a test related in some way to the risks of the failure mode that the test is designed to cover? That may be so – an assessment of risk (quantified or not) is a consideration in the value of tests. But we still have a problem.

Given a valuable test, is a second test that does something similar just as valuable as the first? Not usually. To discuss that, we need some quantum theory.

The Quantum Theory of Testing

When we perform a test, we obtain some outcome and compare that outcome to some expectation.

- If the outcome matches expectations, it meets, in an incremental way, a user's need or requirement. The test incrementally increases our knowledge and confidence.

- If the outcome does not match expectations, it does not meet, in an incremental way, a user's need or requirement. The test will incrementally increase our knowledge but decrease our confidence (until the system is fixed and re-tested successfully).

Each test generates a discrete quantum of evidence. A yes/no, a true/false a 1 or 0. When all tests are run, we aggregate these quanta of evidence and take a more rounded view of the situation. (This happens in the 'apply test – interpret outcome' loop in the New Model [2] by the way).

The important thing is when we run a test – *it only has value if we learn something we did not know before*. If we learn little or nothing – the test has little or no value. A test that has value is *significant* – its significance in that it increases our knowledge about the system under test. When we need to judge whether two tests are better than one, we must look at the *potential value of the second test and its significance.*

A second test may be valuable on its own but matched with a near duplicate – its significance – and true value – is low. The significance of a test maps directly to the incremental increase in coverage that it provides.

The tester – or at least, the person who designed the test model – is the best judge of whether a test is significant. For any measure of coverage to have meaning, it must always be measured with respect to some test model.

Summary

With that rather academic-sounding discussion behind us, what are we to conclude?

The emerging approaches of DevOps, Continuous Delivery and Shift-Left provide a great opportunity to reduce the problem of poor requirements, to move testing earlier and to find and fix problems with less drama. But the increased use of automation also means it will be easier than ever before to collect data on test outcomes. How are we to take advantage of this opportunity?

We need to create test models that are meaningful to our Stakeholders. In this way, the Stakeholder can recognise the value of the tests we propose. As testers and modellers, we can advise on the significance of these tests – the coverage, if you like – with respect to the models themselves. In this way, we can obtain valuable tests and minimise duplication.

The discussion of value and significance of tests also helps us to better gauge the value of our Test Automation. A difficulty I have seen arise in many Test Automation projects is where a complete system test is scoped for automation. When first run as functional tests, they had value. But where these tests are run repeatedly as regression tests, their significance and therefore value is much reduced.

The goal of (what might be better called) an anti-regression test [27] is to detect unwanted behaviour after changes are made. It might be that only 10% of your system tests are necessary to raise the alarm, so to speak. The other 90% cover the same ground and are not significant in this respect.

The goal of this Chapter is to help you to have more informed, better reasoned discussions about decision-making, how much testing is enough and the value of what you do as testers. Relativity and quantum theory might be useful to you after all.

9 A Final Word

Digital is Different

In this little book, I have tried to describe the Digital phenomenon in a non-technical way because Digital, typically, is a business-led initiative. But the challenges and risks, beyond the cultural changes required, are mostly technical.

The novelty, ambition and complexity of some of the systems that are being built now extend beyond our testing abilities. In some respects, the challenges are 'simply' ones of scale – all we need to do is test bigger data volumes, user populations and cloud-based architectures. We can cope with scale relatively easily.

But some systems are so different and so complex in terms of user and system interactions, we will need to design tests that are meaningful and viable at scale. In this sense, scale relates to the number and diversity of scenarios that we must cover in our tests. In the past, we could pick the highest risk and the highest volume scenarios and work with those alone.

But it seems that IoT systems may have a different risk profile. There are millions of scenarios that are all equally likely and risky. We can't use the same risk model to prioritise. We certainly need some new techniques for designing tests and we need new test models and tools to generate test data at volume.

Digital is changing everything.

Assurance in the Digital World

The change that Digital forces on testers and Assurance is profound:

- We need to re-think how we approach testing so that we achieve levels of confidence in very challenging circumstances.

- We need short-cuts to create tests at volume and this requires both superior modelling skills and tools that support modelling too.

- We need our testers to skill up. They need to presume that they test functionality at scale and with tools almost all the time. The days of manual testing in Digital are numbered.

- We need our testing to align precisely with definition and development processes – to Shift-Left, to embed and align with developers, to be indispensable partners in the thinking, development and testing processes.

The New Model for Testing [2] is an attempt to identify the distinct thought processes involved in exploring Sources of Knowledge and the system under test and to scope, design and select meaningful and valuable tests of systems.

I strongly believe that the key to better testing is not better process or more sophisticated tools. Rather it is the interpersonal, communication and thinking skills of testers. If the role of Assurance is to increase the chances of Digital System success, then the person or team doing Assurance must acquire and exhibit the very best of those same skills.

If you are involved in the Digital domain in the capacity of Testing or Assurance, I wish you the best of luck in your projects.

Appendices

References

1. The Tester's Pocketbook, Paul Gerrard, http://testers-pocketbook.com
2. "A New Model for Testing", Paul Gerrard, http://dev.sp.qa/download/newModel
3. Risk-Based E-Business Testing, Paul Gerrard and Neil Thompson, (riskbasedtesting.com, free chapter), 2002
4. "Software Testing Techniques", Boris Beizer, 1990
5. "Lessons Learned in Software Testing", Kaner, Bach, Pettichord, 2002
6. "Courage and Ambition in Teaching and Learning", http://blog.gerrardconsulting.com/?q=node/654
7. The W-Model, http://blog.gerrardconsulting.com/?q=node/531
8. 'Crossing the Chasm' and other books by Geoffrey A Moore, http://www.chasminstitute.com/
9. Continuous Delivery definition, Martin Fowler, http://martinfowler.com/bliki/ContinuousDelivery.html
10. 'Digital Transformation, Testing and Automation', Paul Gerrard's blog, http://blog.gerrardconsulting.com/?q=node/660
11. 'The Laws of Software Process', Philip G Armour.
12. Webinar: 'Agile Test Strategy', Paul Gerrard, http://blog.gerrardconsulting.com/?q=node/627
13. "What is DevOps", The Agile Admin, http://theagileadmin.com/what-is-devops/
14. "Frequency Reduces Difficulty", Martin Fowler, http://martinfowler.com/bliki/FrequencyReducesDifficulty.html

15. "Testing and Checking Refined", James Bach, Michael Bolton, http://www.satisfice.com/blog/archives/856

16. "A New Model for Testing", Paul Gerrard, http://dev.sp.qa/download/newModel

17. "How to Eliminate Manual Feature Checking", Paul Gerrard webinar, http://blog.gerrardconsulting.com/?q=node/622

18. "Thinking Big: Introducing Test Analytics", Paul Gerrard, http://blog.gerrardconsulting.com/?q=node/630

19. The Internet of Everything – What is it and how will it affect you? Paul Gerrard, http://gerrardconsulting.com/sites/default/files/IoEWhatIsIt2.pdf

20. Internet of Everything – Architecture and Risks, Paul Gerrard, http://gerrardconsulting.com/sites/default/files/IoEArchitectureRisks.pdf

21. Internet of Everything – Test Strategy, Paul Gerrard, http://gerrardconsulting.com/sites/default/files/IoETestStrategy.pdf

22. An Overview of High Volume Automated Testing, Cem Kaner, http://kaner.com/?p=278

23. Thinking Big: Introducing Test Analytics, Paul Gerrard, http://blog.gerrardconsulting.com/?q=node/630

24. The Mobile Analytics Playbook, Julian Harty, Antoine Aymer, http://www.themobileanalyticsplaybook.com/

25. http://opensignal.com/reports/2015/08/android-fragmentation/

26. History of Python - Gource - development visualization, https://www.youtube.com/watch?v=cNBtDstOTmA

27. Four papers on Anti-Regression and Test Automation, http://gerrardconsulting.com/?q=node/479

28. "The New Model and Testing v Checking", Paul Gerrard, http://blog.gerrardconsulting.com/?q=node/659

Index

Further Information

Contacting the Author

Should you have any questions or wish to discuss any of the issues raised in this Pocketbook, or perhaps you would like help in improving development or testing in your organisation, please feel free to contact me.

Email: paul@gerrardconsulting.com

Are You Interested in Training?

Gerrard Consulting has provided training courses since 1992. We have a one day tutorial covering the material in this book but also have classes in their topics:

- Exploratory Testing (1 or 2 days with lots of hands on)
- Software Test Automation (1 day exploratory workshop)
- Python Programming (1 or 2 day introduction)
- Modelling, test design and testing (1 or 2 days)
- Surveying and Testing with bot support (under development 1-2 days)

We have a large amount of other training and presentation material and are happy to construct custom courses.

Mentoring and Coaching

Paul is also an independent non-exec adviser, mentor and coach. Get in touch if you think there is a role you he could perform.

CA Technologies

Our Mission: "We eliminate the barriers between ideas and business outcomes."

Copies of this pocketbook can be obtained from CA Incorporated ONLY.

Additional copies can be ordered using this link:

http://transform.ca.com/digital-assurance-advanced-copy.html"

Contact Us

http://www.ca.com/us/company/contact-us.html

www.ingramcontent.com/pod-product-compliance
Lightning Source LLC
Chambersburg PA
CBHW060948050326
40689CB00012B/2598